KIDS GET LEARNING

First published 2022 by Books Boost Business

Tyler is passionate about helping save Rhinos and Elephants so 10% of his profits he donates to this ENDANGERED BLACK RHINO & ELEPHANT CONSERVATION.

3 Tips for Aliens

What is Ho'oponopono?
Written By Tyler David

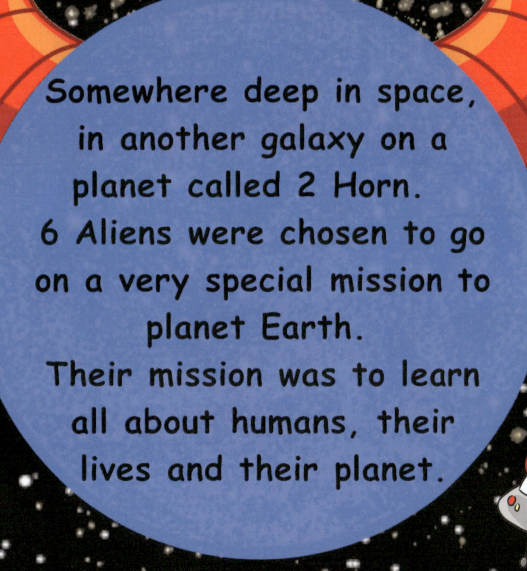

Somewhere deep in space,
in another galaxy on a
planet called 2 Horn.
6 Aliens were chosen to go
on a very special mission to
planet Earth.
Their mission was to learn
all about humans, their
lives and their planet.

Meet the team.

This Spaceship is hidden on every page
for you to find.

Your Human

Your pet will love to learn ho'oponopono together.

Step 1

You and your pet can take a deep breath.

Breathe into your heart.

Step 2

Be together, gently head to head.

Heart to heart, or looking into their eyes.

Step 3

Then say these magic words to each other.

Be a great pet owner and teach your human ho'oponopono.

Fun things to do
Spot the 5 Differences

Colour me in

Draw the H

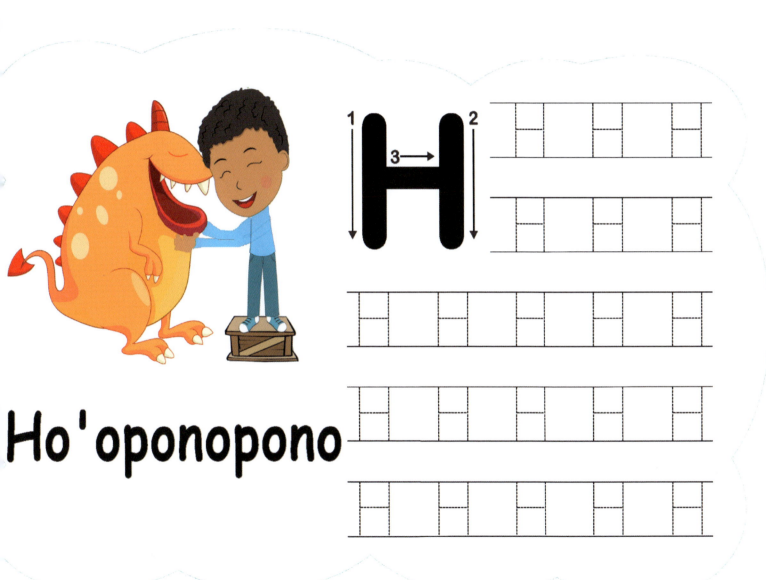

Ho'oponopono

Rhyming words

Love

Magic

Dove

Above

Words

Glove

If you enjoyed this book please look out for my other books by searching "3 Tips for Aliens" on Amazon

Thank you for your support I am really grateful.

More books from Tyler David

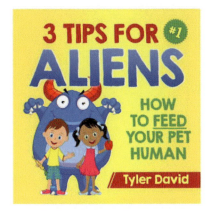

This book is a great fun way for kids to learn all about healthy eating and drinking, to learn what is good for their bodies. this is suitable for all, vegetarians, vegans, gluten free and other allergies. Using whole foods and organic produce.

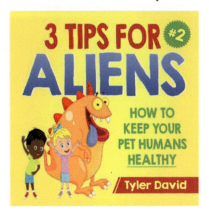

A fun way for your child to learn about exercise and moving their bodies. Written by a child for children. Tyler (age 5) is passionate about helping kids be healthy and strong, So they have plenty of time to play and be happy. Including fun activities.

Tyler's first ever book! Tyler David the little boy with a huge heart for adventure. Takes you on a fun journey in his first ever book. A super fun read for you and your children to share.

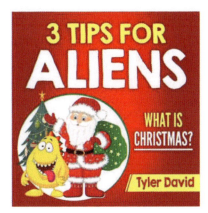

A fun way for your child to learn all about Christmas. Written by a child for children. Tyler (age 5) is passionate about learning all the fun times of year. So kids have plenty of time to plan, play and be happy. Including fun activities.
Part of a series

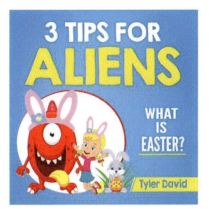

A fun way for your child to learn all about Easter.
Written by a child for children. Tyler (age 5) is passionate about learning all the fun times of year. So they have plenty of time to plan, play and be happy. Including fun activities.
Part of a series

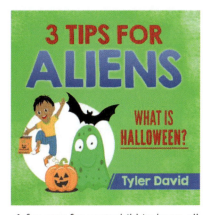

A fun way for your child to learn all about Halloween.
Written by a child for children. Tyler (age 5) is passionate about learning all the fun times of year. So they have plenty of time to plan, play and be happy. Including fun activities.
Part of a series

KIDS GET LEARNING

Printed in Great Britain
by Amazon